International Postalcodes Llisted

M. B. Thomas

copyright 2010/06/04

:

PREFACE

Mails have been missing because of use of invalid postal codes; people have been denied services because they could not submit valid zip or postal codes; jobs have been lost because of want of postal or zip codes.

In this information communication technology (ICT) age, virtually no person-to-person, distant business transaction can be carried out without post or zip codes.

As we all know, goods can not be delivered through internet or intranets but through our contact addresses or shipping addresses, these addresses are tracked through postal codes.

This booklet deals solely with international postal/zip codes. Some countries have, some do not use while some have changed their postal/zip codes over the years whereas some use moiré than one. However, this compilation is just an updated list some countries' old code that is no more in use has been discarded in this compilation. Those who still use both their old codes with their new ones have both codes listed in this booklet.

Mannie Thomas
2010/06/04.

LIST OF INTERNATIONAL POSTAL CODES

1. Åland

(AX-)99999

2. Albania:

(AL-)9999.

3. Algeria:

99999

4. American Samoa:

99999 or 99999-9999

5. Andorra:

AD999

Angola:

NIL

Anguilla:

AI-2640.

6. Antigua and Barbuda:

NIL

7. Argentina:

A9999AAA.

8. Armenia:

9999

9. Aruba:

No postal codes used.

10. Ascension Island:

ASCN 1ZZ..

11. Australia:

9999

12. **Austria:**

(A- or AT-)9999

13. **Azerbaijan:**

AZ9999

14. **Bahamas:**

NIL

15. **Bahrain:**

999 or 9999.

16. **Bangladesh:**

9999

17. **Barbados**

BB99999

18. **Belarus: (BY)**

999999

19. **Belgium: (B- or BE-)**

9999

20. Belize:

NIL

21. Benin:

NIL

22. Bermuda:

AA 99

23. Bhutan:

NIL

24. Bolivia:

9999

25. Bosnia and
Herzegovina:

(BA-)99999

26. Botswana:

NIL

27. **Brazil:**

99999-999

28. **British Antarctic Territory:**

BIQQ 1ZZ

29. **British Indian Ocean Territory**

: BBND 1ZZ

30. **British Virgin Islands:**

VG9999

31. **Brunei:**

AA9999

32. **Bulgaria:**

(BG-)9999

33. **Burkina Faso:**

NIL

34. Burundi:

NIL

35. Cambodia:

99999

36. Cameroon:

NIL

37. Canada:

A9A 9A9.

38. Cape Verde:

9999

39. Cayman Islands:

KY9-9999

40. **Central African Republic:**

NIL

41. **Chad:**

99999

42. **Chile:**

9999999

43. **China, People's Republic of (Mainland):**

999999

44. **Christmas Island:**

9999

45. **Cocos (Keeling) Island:**

9999

46. **Colombia:**

999999 '

47. Comoros:

NIL

48. Congo (Brazzaville):

NIL

49. Congo, Democratic Republic:

NIL

50. Cook Islands:

NIL

51. Costa Rica:

99999

52. Côte d'Ivoire:

NIL

53. Croatia:

(HR-)99999

54. Cuba:

99999.

55. Cyprus:

(CY-)9999

56. Czech Republic:

(CZ-)99999

57. Denmark:

(DK-)9999

58. Djibouti:

NIL

59. Dominica:

NIL

60. Dominican Republic:

99999

61. East Timor:

NIL

62. Ecuador:

EC999999

63. Egypt

99999

64. El Salvador:

9999

65. Equatorial Guinea:

NIL

66. Eritrea:

NIL.

67. Estonia:

(EE-)99999

68. Ethiopia:

9999

69. Falkland Islands:

FIQQ 1ZZ

70. Faroe Islands:

(FO-)999

71. Federated States of Micronesia:

99999

72. Fiji:

NIL

73. Finland:

(FI-)99999.

74. France:

(F-)99999

75. Gabon:

99 [city name] 99

76. Gambia:

NIL

77. Georgia:

(GE-)9999

78. Germany:

99999

79. Gibraltar:

NIL

80. Greece:

(GR-)99999

81. Greenland:

(DK-)9999

82. Grenada:

NIL.

83. Guam:

99999

84. **Guatemala:**

99999.

85. **Guernsey:**

**GY9 9AA or
GY99 9AA**

86. **Guyana:**

NIL

87. **Haiti:**

(HT-)9999

88. **Heard and McDonald
Islands:**

9999

89. **Honduras:**

99999

90. **Hong Kong:**

999077

91. Hungary:

(H- or HU-)9999

92. Iceland:

(IS-)999

93. India:

999 999

94. Indonesia:

99999

95. Iran:

99999 99999

96. Iraq:

99999

97. Ireland:

NIL

98.   Isle of Man:

IM9 9AA or IM99 9AA

99.   Israel:

99999

100. Italy:

99999

101. Jamaica: Previously

JMAAA99

102. Japan:

999-9999

103. Jersey:

JE9 9AA or JE99 9AA

104. Kazakhstan:

999999

105. Kenya:

99999.

106. Kiribati:

MIL.

107. Korea, North:

NIL.

108. Korea, South:

999-999

109. Kosovo:

99999

110. Kuwait:

99999

111. Kyrgyzstan:

999999: (LV-)9999

112. Laos:

99999

113. Lebanon:

9999 in rural areas,

9999 9999 in urban areas.

114. Lesotho:

999

115. Liberia:

9999

116. Libya:

99999

117. Liechtenstein:

(FL- or LI-)9999.

118. Lithuania:

(LT-)99999

119. Luxembourg:

(L- or LU-)9999

120. Macau:

999078

121. Macedonia:

(MK-)9999

122. Madagascar:

999

123. Malawi:

NIL.

124. Maldives:

99-99

125. Malaysia:

99999

126. Mali:

NIL

127. Malta:

AAA 9999

128. Marshall Islands:

99999 or 99999-9999

129. Mauritania:

NIL

130. Mauritius:

NIL.

131. Mexico:

99999.

132. Moldova:

(MD-)9999

133. Monaco:

(MC-)99999

134. Mongolia:

999999

135. Montenegro:

(ME-)99999

136. Montserrat:

NIL.

137. Morocco:

99999

138. Mozambique:

99999

139. Myanmar:

99999

140. Namibia:

NIL

141. Nauru:

NIL

142. Nepal:

99999

143. Netherlands:

(NL-)9999 AA.

144. Netherlands Antilles:

NIL

145. New Zealand:

9999

146. Nicaragua:

999-999-9

147. Niger:

9999

148. Nigeria:

999999

149. Niue:

NIL

150. Norfolk Island:

9999

151. Northern Mariana Islands:

99999 or 99999-9999

152. Norway:

(NO-)9999.

153. Oman:

999

154. Palau:

99999

155. Pakistan:

99999

156. Panama:

NIL

157. Papua New Guinea:

999

158. Paraguay:

9999

159. Peru:

99

160. Philippines:

9999

161. Pitcairn Islands:

PCRN 1ZZ

162. Poland:

(PL-)99-999

163. Portugal:

(PT-)9999-999

164. Puerto Rico:

99999 or 99999-9999

165. Qatar:

NIL

166. Romania:

(RO-)999999

167. Russia:

999999

168. Rwanda:

NIL

169. San Marino:

(SM-)99999..

170. Saint Helena:

STHL 1ZZ

171. Saint Kitts and Nevis:

NIL

172. Saint Lucia:

NIL

173. Saint Vincent and the Grenadines:

NIL

174. Sao Tome and Principe:

NIL

175. Saudi Arabia:

99999

176. Senegal:

99999

177. Serbia:

(RS-)99999

178. Seychelles:

NIL

179. Sierra Leone:

NIL

180. Singapore:

999999

181. Solomon Islands:

NIL.

182. Somalia:

NIL

183. South Africa:

9999

184. South Georgia and the South Sandwich Islands:

SIQQ 1ZZ

185. Slovakia:

(SK-)999 99

186. Slovenia:

(SI-)9999

187. Spain: (E- or

ES-)99999

188. Sri Lanka:

99999Sudan: 9999

189. Suriname:

NIL.

190. Swaziland:

A999

191. Sweden:

(SE-)999 99

192. Switzerland:

(CH-)9999

193. Syria:

NIL

194. Taiwan:

99999

195. Tajikistan:

(TJ-)999999

196. Tanzania:

MIL

197. Thailand:

99999

198. Tokelau:

NIL

199. Tonga:

NIL

200. Trinidad and Tobago:

NIL

201. Tristan da Cunha:

TDCU 1ZZ

202. Tunisia:

9999

203. Turkey:

(TR-)99999

204. Turkmenistan:

999999

205. Turks and Caicos Islands:

TKCA 1ZZ

206. Tuvalu:

NIL

207. Uganda:

NIL

208. Ukraine:

99999

209. United Arab Emirates:

NIL

210. United Kingdom:

A9 9AA, A99 9AA, A9A 9AA, AA9 9AA, AA99 9AA, or AA9A 9AA.

211. United States of America: (known as the ZIP Code)

99999 or 99999-9999

212. Uruguay:

99999

213. US Virgin Islands:

99999 or 99999-9999

214. Uzbekistan:

999999

215. Vanuatu:

NIL.

216. Vatican City:

(VA-)00120.

217. Venezuela:

9999. 9999 A

218. Vietnam:

999999

219. Yemen:

NIL

220. Zambia:

99999.

221. Zimbabwe:

NIL

222. Afghanistan:

NIL

www.ingramcontent.com/pod-product-compliance
Lightning Source LLC
Chambersburg PA
CBHW071319280526
45788CB00004B/1942